The Life Worth Living Series

A Series on How to Live the Life of Christ He Promised Us, The Abiding Life With the Voice of the Lord Restored and Leading You in Every Step.

Rev. James J Cucuzza

ISBN: 149615004X
ISBN 13: 9781496150042
Library of Congress Control Number: 2014904305
CreateSpace Independent Publishing Platform
North Charleston, South Carolina

I

The Life Worth Living

There is only one way to the life worth living. It doesn't look the same for everyone naturally, but the way to that life is the same. This life is described in the Bible as the *"life of the Spirit in Christ"* (Romans 8:1-14).

God makes it clear just how to obtain this life through the example of Jesus Christ. Simply put, Jesus lived His life for all to see and more importantly made the way for all of us to be able to live our life as He did. (I John 2:6) He was the *"Prototype"*. Notice, I didn't say, 'live His life', but 'have the same system of living that He had.' He said that He was the way.

I believe this is the life that is described as *"Completion"* or *"Perfection"* in the Word of God. (Ephesians 4:12). This simply means *"having all the necessary parts"*. In essence, it means to be made into His likeness as a son of God. How do we obtain this life and how do we apply this life to our own everyday lives? These are the questions that we will answer.

WHAT WE NEED TODAY ARE SOME ANSWERS

God has always and is always speaking. What is He saying? What is He doing now? What is He about to do? What are the requirements we must meet for that life He created us for to come about? Are we ready to meet the requirements? Can we meet some of the requirements ignorantly and enjoy somewhat of a good life sporadically or can we meet those requirements deliberately and gain a *life worth living?* I believe we can!!!

There is a vast difference between just good teaching and a *life giving* Word from God that informs, inspires and empowers us to live the life we are talking about. God can use information, but He first must breathe on it with His Spirit before it becomes a word that empowers us to do His will. In order for that to happen, it needs to be relevant to life itself.

WE ARE MOVING INTO THE CONCLUSION OF THIS AGE

The last two thousand years we have been in the age of the church. Yes, we experienced the reformation; however, I believe He still desires to further reform the church as an institution to its original mission to people. I believe the church has never experienced, even in the past great revivals, the fullness of moving on to what is described in the word of God as *perfection* or *completion,* and the time is now at hand.

The final harvest is upon us and it behooves us to know what to do. Unless people are brought to this *Perfection* or *Completion,* we will never reap the harvest God wants. (Ephesians 5:11) The reason is His people must come into their own purpose individually, walking as Jesus Christ walked in order to reach His intended people. This isn't just about what He did, but how He did it!! Finding our purpose is one thing, being able to live it out is another.

What is hindering us from moving on? How will complete success in this walk look and how do we reach that success? Just what is going on??? What should be going on??? These are the questions we will examine and try to answer. Our message will be a message that continually points to the Holy Spirit and away from the self-sufficiency of man and religion. I believe for the sake of the coming great harvest, He is giving us clear answers to these questions. Why now, because it's just His time!!!

When man leans on his own understanding and power, it creates a *"loosing cycle"* of self-inflicted trouble. We are doomed to repeat this cycle, if we don't get our paradigm right. We are looking for more than just change in the church; we are looking to change the entire world system. It's an insurmountable vision, but we believe it is God's vision and He will empower us to accomplish it!!

Let's not just get a *"second wind"* for His people, let's get resurrection power!! Let's go on to perfection and the *"Life worth living"*!!!

II

The Time We are In

Because of the rapid changes in our society; people are experiencing many "failed expectations" in life. Things just are not turning out the way we have thought. This leads to depression. Depression is at an all-time high. As a result, depression has covered the nation like a wet blanket. We see it everywhere.

God's people have yet to display the one thing He promised, peace and rest. A rest from the inside out, not some place you go to or something that has to happen for us. I'm talking about the kind of peace and rest described all throughout the Bible. It's the very Promised Land earmarked for God's people.

Something has been left out, something is very wrong and we believe we have some answers. Not just what it is, but how to obtain it!!! The pattern is right before our eyes in the Bible. This was the mission of Jesus Christ as the son of God, to reveal this pattern and provide the way to it. He said: "*I am the way, the truth, and the LIFE*".

We need to reach the desired outcome of the Christian faith, THE VERY LIKENESS OF CHRIST. In the book of I Peter 1:11, Peter described it as "*Perfection*". This includes freedom from *fears, agitating passions and moral conflicts*. He goes on to say: "*We need to reach the end of our faith, the salvation of our souls*". This is the goal and object of the salvation package Christ obtained for us. This salvation goes beyond the spirit to our very souls, our will, mind and emotions.

THE PROBLEM NOW

Today we are overwhelmed with information. We are inundated with information on how to live the best life. After all, if we need the facts, can't we just *"Google"* and find it? Just about anything we desire can be google searched. Why not that? Science, medicine and even religion all believe they have the answer to our problems. No, as effective as they are, God has the answers, and He has written His will both in nature and society. What we need to know is how do we line up and harmonize with His will. The first thing He told us to pray is *"Thy will be done"*. When this is our prayer, He can take it from there.

We are trained early on in life to look externally for the answers and secondly, to gaze internally. Our first thought is maybe we just need more information. All the information we need is instantly available to us via our computer or smart phone. It gives us a sense of control over circumstances and therefore offers us security. It will fail. Like Verizon's new motto this year, *"a new year, a new you"*. Your smartphone will create a new you! One more promise from another giant!! Not so!!

We have so much information; we no longer need to rely on our own memory, intuition or the voice of God. In this may lie what is wrong in society and it has been wrong for a very long time!! I believe it is! Google and other search engines are like the tree of the knowledge of good and evil, that deceptive tree spoken of in the Bible in the book of Genesis. It's been around a long, long time!!

This tree or bank of information allows us to rely on our own understanding and minimizes our need to tap into the voice of God. Therefore we think we don't need Him to live life. It seems the more information we get, the further away we get from what we need and want to know most; how to hear the voice of God. This voice is what tells us how to live the life worth living. All this information has crippled our own minds and made us dependent on it for survival and a sense of control over our lives. We are drowning in our own information!!

The voice of God restored to us is the answer to our problems. Notice in Deuteronomy 28:1 that it is not the law, but the voice that is the answer. The law was only meant to bring us into a better understanding of who God is and what He wants. It also was meant to show us our very shortcomings to fulfilling what He wants. The voice of God restored to our lives is the true way to blessings that overwhelm us as described in this passage. Without it, we have "*no rest for our feet*". (Deuteronomy 28:65)

WE ARE LIKE THE RICH MAN THAT CAME TO JESUS

We, like the rich man portrayed in the Bible, must unfortunately say, "*We have been there and done that*", and continue with the same question, "*What do I still lack?*" (Luke 18:18) Jesus said "*Without Me*" (which means in relationship with me) there is nothing we can do, but "*with Him*" all things are possible.

The rich man was looking to his own resources. The rich man needed the faith that looks to God's resources. After all what did Jesus offer, but a poor miserable servant's life? Why should He look to Him? The rich man marginalized Jesus because of His own pride, arrogance and success. God wants a relationship with us not our success stories. So again like the rich man, we remain frustrated even with our successes.

People of all ages and strata are doing the same thing this rich man did; only in different ways. They are seeking direction to a better life and the power to realize and secure it. What they sometimes don't realize is that they need to be seeking a return to God's original intent and purpose.

Do we have the power to fulfill this purpose? The law of the Old Testament Bible (sometimes called the manual for the human) only brings with it the knowledge of our shortcomings, impotency and sin. We still need the power to avoid the failure the law reveals in our lives. Like a car without an engine, we just can't get to where we are going. Why? I believe it's our paradigm. It needs to be changed.

WE TREAT SYMPTOMS AND DO NOT ELIMINATE CAUSE OR SEEK THE CURE

We are using "*placebos*" both in society and the church for our problems. The church has its own "placebos". The results are like we hear on TV. We are told the devastating side effects of drugs which often create new problems. Our last state is worse than our first!!

The church, in general, would call the root cause for our failures sin; and we treat this with the law, discipline and self-effort. We treat it with "*outside influence*" to encourage, or threaten and somehow satisfy this hunger for a new way of life. We go right back to the old system with a new resolve in our heart only to find later distraction and failure. The results still bring the same consequences with them. Paul, the Apostle, addressed this in the books of Romans and Galatians. He said: "*I have no confidence in the natural man*". (Philippians 3:3)

This striving to rid us of sin leads to failure again and again. This is a losing cycle that has been repeated throughout the history of mankind. The sad thing is that Jesus came to change that and we have not fully understood it.

Both the institutions of religion and the world operate on the same system. It is the operating system of the natural man. We live by our five senses while disconnected from the voice of God. All this leads us to believe that we can do life without a direct connection to the voice of God. And we can to a certain extent, at least in the eyes of the world. The problem is success is only to a certain extent and then what. Failure, over and over again!!! This is the loosing cycle of living life without God's voice.

There is something (other than just sin) hiding at the very depth of the human nature that is wrong, long before sin ever comes in with its final blows. I believe like others, I know what it is. Unlike others, I'm going to commit my life to explaining how to reveal this root problem and how to cure it; then maybe we can go on to Perfection or Completion.

Our Christian teaching missed some of the original intent Jesus had in His teaching, but it is the most important teaching He gave us. It was His very mission to show us. He provided for the change in us through His blood, cross and resurrection; and we have missed the main point. The teaching He gave us shows us how He operated while here on earth.

THE CHURCH IS STILL IN THE REFORMATION PERIOD

Much of the message of the church today has distorted God's original intent for man and replaced His blueprint for living with religion and performance of *"Christian law"*. It's just the same system presented in a religious format. I believe with that said, the effort on the part of all leaders is noble and in most cases honest. I was one of those leaders for many years.

The effects of these distortions and deceptions have been delusional at best and devastating Christian lives for centuries. We can believe the deception that we are all right and doing well. Like a rich man, if we do manage to have a decent life by the world's standards, we become self-satisfied and miss the very thing we were looking for.

There are many people that have, in their own strength, created a good Christian life and achieve acclaim in the church's eyes. Looking good on the outside is equated with the good life we all seek. It's nothing but the same *"fig leaves"* described in Genesis. One look at Jesus though, and our failure becomes obvious.

III

Some Perspectives that Need to Change

What is a paradigm? It's a map we think with. We have many maps in our brains. These give us our perspective on life. If that point of view, position or paradigm changes, all of our perspective changes. It's like the little north arrow on our phones or GPS. It's our "*true north*". We hope it is true north!! We need to develop God's paradigm.

Jesus said be careful "*how you see*, not just what you see scripture"? Like a kaleidoscope, each turn of the dial changes every chip of color (the facts that we see) to something different. The same pieces look totally different from one person to another and sometimes from one time to another.

In turn these perspectives will change our expectations of what is to come. I find my expectations constantly changing and with it my whole attitude changes. This new paradigm is bringing rest and joy to me. Our thoughts and attitudes determine the life we live. On the other hand this is the problem we have today, too many people with too many different ways to look at truth. What turns the truth into a lie is what is in us that effects our ability to see truth in the proper light. We must have the true paradigm; the one Jesus bought for us on the cross and resurrection life.

THE TIME FOR CHANGE IS NOW

We are beginning to realize our own ways, as much as any sin, has hurt us. Our own ways are much different than sin. Our own ways represent the root problem with our lives long before sin becomes a problem. Our own ways stem from our tendency to live apart from the Holy Spirit's influence and power in all our actions.

Our Christian faith includes a fatal blow to this tendency to act apart from God and provides the answer to staying connected to Him. Not just a prayer life, but a walk in the unseen. Jesus provided the way, the cross, and the resurrection!!!

I believe that after centuries of the church age, we are now in the *Day of Atonement*, the small feast before the great Feast of Tabernacles. (Leviticus 23:27).

Atonement among many things means to push the *"reset button".* It deals with shutting down our own self-sufficiency and bringing ourselves into alignment with God's thoughts. It is the last feast preceding the great feast of tabernacles. The feast of tabernacles is the last great harvest at the end of this age. The harvest refers to the people who will repent and return to God. We need this revival!! Revival is a period of time when large groups of people repent and return to God. Throughout history there have been periods of revival followed by seemingly dry spiritual times.

Many Christian leaders are predicting the next revival is at hand. The question is what are we going to revive people to? What does this feast of tabernacles look like? I'm sure this time of being revived is more than just where we have come from. We cannot look back to move forward.

What I see ahead is an unbelievable move of the Holy Spirit, but it will not look like how we have built in the past, and thank God it won't look like it does today!! Yes, He is working and bringing us into Atonement.

WE NEED OUR NEW OPERATING SYSTEM

As the computer we have an operating system we live on. We have been living on this old system from the beginning of this dispensation of time. It is our five senses informing us of our surrounding activities and then responding to them. We are influenced from the outside in. We live responding to outside stimuli.

The five senses give our soul (our mind, emotions and will) information. The soul stands between us (our innermost being or the spirit) and our world. We are spirit, not soul. This place called the soul is the battleground we fight on every day.

From time to time we have been getting some "*upgrades*" to our system, but not much has changed. There seems to be just another *virus* after the last one that pops up. The results are the same. We have Jesus in our heart, we are filled with the Spirit, but the system remains the same. Failure!!

THE GOSPEL PRESENTED NOT JUST A NEW LIFE, BUT FIRST AND FOREMOST, A NEW OPERATING SYSTEM.

We were meant to live and walk "*As Jesus walked in the earth*". (1 John 2:10). "*As*" here means on the system He lived on, not just the very same works He performed. We have our own work to do, but the system is the same as His. The result is as He said: "*I only do those things I see the Father do*".

The whole world needs this new system. We are reaching the end of this age and I believe we are going to be introduced to this way of life. It was in the Bible all along. It is called "*completion*" or "*perfection*". The result is that it restores those who are willing to operate this way to the voice of God. He then brings rest from inside, as the Scripture puts it being free from "*agitating passions, fear and moral conflicts*". (I Peter) Paul, the apostle, desired and gave his entire life to present every man and woman as complete. (Colossians 1:28).

THE GOAL OF "*THE LIFE WORTH LIVING*"

The goal of this book is to introduce people to the needed paradigm changes which finally brings God's people to completion. It is intended to restore us to the garden experience and most importantly the voice of God. It is intended to bring us into harmony with God and the rest promised us. All of us want to live "*the life worth living*" (Proverbs 3:1, 2 amp)

We want a life that reflects the promises of God, a blessed life, which reflects the resulting success to others. Our life should cause others to want to know our God and Father. Our life should be an example that attracts others. The gospel is best communicated to others through attraction, not promotion.

As earlier stated, the time is late and we need to move on from where we are as His church to complete the work He has begun in our lives. We have had problems in Christianity with understanding and presenting Christ. Just what did He come to accomplish here on earth for us and through us? We are big on pointing to Him and His work, but small on becoming like Him and letting Him live His life out through us, so His work on earth can be finished.

Let's look at our problem and be willing to see we have come up short of this life in many ways.

IV

What is the Promised Completion

GOD WILL COMPLETE HIS PEOPLE

It is a fact that He will *complete* or *perfect* His people. (Hosea 1:1) His purpose is for us to be conformed into His "*expressed*" image. (Hebrews 1:3). In (Ephesians 4:11), it speaks of the "*completeness*" and "*stature*" that Jesus walked in and our call to walk as He did. Simply put, completeness literally means *having all the necessary parts* that He had. It speaks of His people transforming into the likeness of Christ and walking the earth as He did. "*Completion or perfection*" means here in this Scripture that we might be filled "*Plero*" or "*Crammed*" with the completeness of His life. It means to come to His maturity and His stature; in other words, it's time to grow up!

The first reason to be complete is to keep us from being "*blown around by different winds of life and false mentalities*". It literally means to "*Push, or Hurl us around*". Have you ever been hurled around by life's events, while hanging onto old mentalities? Completion insulates us from outside influence. This completion will also prepare us to do the work of serving those God has chosen and to build up His body, the church on earth.

Living as Christ was always meant to be achieved by God's people. It was God's intent and purpose for us. He sent Jesus to show us the way and to be the way. Yes, there is a process, but a process that brings us to His full stature. It seems oftentimes the church has majored on the process and lost its bearings to reach the goal. What could be going wrong? I believe in every case it is the deception of religion, man's efforts to attain to the life God has for us depending on our natural state. It is efforts that are based on our own abilities and efforts to bring forth a life that is like Christ's, *"the life worth living"*.

THE *"DELAY"*, THE DIVERSION, *"THE MYSTERY"*

In the book of Revelation, it says there has been a delay until the end of this age. (Revelation 10) It isn't that God was pleased with the delay, but it is in fact a delay. I believe it is time for us to move forward, simply because He is now revealing the causes for the delay and presenting to us the way to move toward completion.

In Colossians 2:18, the writer states that we, as Christians, have been *"defrauded of our reward"*. We have been robbed of the life that Christ has always had for us, the life that reflects that *"completion"* or *"perfection"* the Bible talks about.

We have been robbed by two things: by a false humility (putting ourselves lower than we should) and by the worship of angels. These two subjects are what have hindered the church from coming into the full stature of Christ.

First let us address just who are the angels. Often we make angels more important than man. In Hebrews 1:1, the Scripture addresses this problem by stating that we were created at a lower level for a little while, but we are of a higher position than the angels. Angels were specifically created to be *"ministers"* or servants to those who would come later and obtain salvation, those who actually would inherit the promises of God, the life of Christ and live as He did in the earth. Angels were in a word *helpers* for us to reach this goal. Then the world would be restored to its original form.

In the book of Hebrews, it says *"we were made a little lower, for a little while than the angels, until He has put all things under mankind's feet"* (Hebrews 1). John, the apostle, said it this way, *"it doesn't yet appear what we will be, but we do see Jesus"*. His intention was to *"bring many to glory"*. What does glory mean here? Simply put, it means His likeness. We are to grow up and look and act more and more like Jesus.

When Peter was on the mountain, Jesus changed into what He really was on the inside out; and Peter received just a glimpse of what it's like to receive complete salvation. His image was so glorious that all they could do was fall down like they were dead. (Matthew 17) Peter, later on in life, talks of completion and refers to his experience on the mountain. He saw it!!
(1 Peter)

At Bethlehem the angels were so excited, when Christ was born, they said *"Glory to God in the Highest"*; and the second part is even more dramatic, *"Peace on earth and good will toward men"*. Why, because they had been without an ability to fulfill their purpose and the way to a better life had arrived through this new born baby. They had been, if you will, *"in the unemployment line"*. They had been waiting for mankind to become what they were supposed to become so they could do the job they were created to do. They were to serve mankind in this great effort of completion and perfection. I say, 'Hallelujah!!'

V

Pressing on From the Book of Hebrews

WE HAVE BEEN NEGLECTING THE REAL ISSUE

We see the second reason in Hebrews 2:11 for being defrauded of our reward. We have been *"neglecting"* or *"marginalizing"* the salvation we are called to. The definition of *"neglecting"* is to *ignore, forget, overlook* and more importantly to *avoid* something. We have been ignoring at best, and avoiding at worst, the real issue at hand. Salvation in this Scripture means to accomplish *"conversion"* to our intended form as God's sons, Christ's life Himself.

Of course each of our lives will look different outwardly because of our call in life. We are called to different areas of life. But what does it mean is to live as He did then? We live in the same way; whatever we do. I believe it has more to do with what *"operating system"* and power we live in rather than just what we do. We are going to answer this question as to how He lived so that we can walk as He walked.

One of the problems in the church is the way we use our terminology. We need to redefine our terms that we have been using in the church. Often our leaders (including myself) have, so to speak, *"stunted God's people's growth"* through this terminology. We use terms like *converted, saved, spirit-filled* and even *Christian* in a way that gives us the impression we have arrived at where God has intended us to be. We got it all; we have reached the finish line.

Some people stop at different places along the way to complete salvation thinking they have fulfilled all the requirements of a good life. Some have arrived at different levels of salvation and because of these accomplishments along the way, they are so excited. They are led to think it is the whole package. Some people for instance have the truth, but not the life, and yet again, some have the life and the truth, but not the way. But we need all three to have the complete package of salvation. Jesus said he was *the way, the truth and the life*.

What I desire to discuss is the one very important missing link to the complete salvation package. Peter said it in I Peter 1:9 concerning completion, *"receiving the end of our faith the salvation of our souls"*. Boy we need a lot of faith for that!! Peter did also.

It goes on in Hebrews 3:1 to say *"let us consider the apostle Jesus Christ"*. In considering Jesus, we are considering ourselves also because we too are begotten of the Father. What are the two traits of Jesus mentioned here? He was *appointed* and He was *faithful*. (Matthew 8:14) Why, because He had received not only the truth, and the way, but the life God has for all of us.

"TODAY IF YOU HEAR HIS VOICE"

In (Hebrews 3:11, the writer goes on to encourage the people not to give up on this salvation. Don't harden your heart!! Don't give up!! Don't ignore it!! God was displeased with them for their lack of faith to achieve the Promised Land which represented Christ's life. It was a life of rest and success in every area. Even though they were on the brink of obtaining it all, they grew disinterested and gave up. They did not *"perceive"* or *"recognize"* His ways and complained about the journey. They tested God more than He did them, but it says that God *stood the test with them*. The good news is,: that although they did not enter in, He has made and given us a better way in which we can enter that Promised Land!! In saying *"Today"* repeatedly He is saying that time has not run out!!

It goes on to say they did not get *progressively better*. They "s*ettled*" into rebellion. They left the beginning of their faith and ran out of energy to obtain that life. Have you ever been there? In Hebrews 10:32, it says that *"they refused to be persuaded."* Persuaded simply means to be *"affected, influenced, swayed, inspired, altered, and adjusted."*

WE NEED TO BE AFRAID OF ONE THING, TO DISTRUST THE PROMISE

The writer again exhorts us in Hebrews 4:1 to *"be afraid to distrust the promise"*. It's not too late to start over while it is called *"Today"*. Every day the Bible reads, *"Today if you will hear My voice"*. Today means every day so there is a chance to obtain this salvation every day that we are still alive, no matter what the day may bring. The Scripture says in Lamentations 3:23 *"His mercies are new every morning"*.

It also goes on to say that even though they didn't have the faith to go to the Promised Land they could have. But they did not choose to join Joshua and Caleb who believed for the Promised Land and finally went into the land. They missed the opportunity because they lacked faith.

When you are down and you're thinking it's time to give up, don't be like those who died in the desert; who refused to join up with those who were going in. You can join up with people who have faith. They will carry you with their faith. Stay in relationship with people who have a mind to enter into all God has for them.

Find someone that is determined to get into the land. Even though Caleb and Joshua did not have the make-up to stay there, at least they got their foot in the door. And what went wrong with them that they did not obtain the promise? We can know what it is and avoid their demise, why, because of the new covenant that Jesus came to give us. They spiraled downward into a *"loosing cycle"* as we see through the entire book of Judges. It is the same loosing cycle we find ourselves in today, because we do not understand fully the *"horn of salvation"* that Jesus came to give us, but we will now.

FOR THE WORD WILL HELP YOU

In Hebrews 4:11, the writer goes on to say *"for the Word of God will help you"*. How does the Word help us? It will reveal how we are handling our circumstances by *exposing, shifting, analyzing, and judging them*. Jesus was the pattern and was *"in all points tempted as we are"*. That means we can look at how He handled each one.

I want to know how I'm handling problems along the way to perfection and the adjustments necessary to correct any problems or deficiencies I have. I want to be tested. James says the *"testing of our faith is more precious than gold* (James 1). It's because He has the answers and the power to change us in the new covenant.

The writer of Hebrews writes on and says something was going wrong. It's still going wrong today. There was a delay in the people obtaining this salvation that was to be so glorious. When he desired to go on and teach at this point in the book, he could not find the words to teach with. It was hard to get the anointing to teach them and could not proceed in teaching. He wanted to see them go on to completion or perfection and could not. What was the problem?

DEFINING WHAT WENT WRONG

The problem is they had become *dull, sluggish, and slothful at achieving spiritual sight*. They were unskilled in the *"doctrine of righteousness"*. (Hebrews 5:11-13) Righteousness means the way!! What is that? It is the right way and purpose of God to enter into the Promised Land. It was ignorance of the system of living. Christ came to demonstrate the system of living and more importantly lead us into it.

The writer of Hebrews goes on and begins to teach on Melchizedek, the priest, as a pattern for us and finally stops midway and says this: what goes here??? He goes on to say they had not gone on to maturity. Simply put: *"They also did not become conformed to the divine will, purpose and thought"*.

Today there are countless Christians in our churches, although they look good, act pretty good and are affirmed as good members, they have come short and have become sluggish, at best, and slothful, at worst, in becoming transformed into God's image. They apply law and religious standards to their lives and clean up on the outside in their own strength. They continue to live influenced by outside circumstances. They rely on their five human senses.

They have not been *"trained by practice to go on to completion or perfection into the expressed image of Christ"*. Trained here means to *"exert energy towards achieving it, to work out, repeat, drill and go over, and duplicate."* It also means *"to distinguish, detect, and discern the way to this land of rest."* What was it? The writer of Hebrews mentions here they did not have their spiritual senses trained. There are a new set of senses that we receive when we receive the Holy Spirit; why, because He, the Holy Spirit is a person also, not just a power like so many think. He senses all we do and He is in us!! And He has a say in all of it!! Oh My!! The voice!!

LET US GET PAST

Now the writer of Hebrews comes with another exhortation. *"Let us get past this elementary stage"*. (Hebrews 6:1) What the Lord is saying to the church is: let's grow up, let's go on, and let's exert the energy to obtain this salvation. The literal meaning here is to *"steadily precede, progress, spring forward, get headway, breakthrough, advance, move forward and do it consistently, persistently and habitually"*.

NO MORE LAYING FAULTY FOUNDATIONS

In Hebrews 6:2-3, the writer is saying let's not have a lot of what I call *"repeat business"* at the altars in our churches praying our way out of life's missteps and problems only to go out the next week and repeat the cycle. We should not be repenting of work and actions that were *"dead"* from the beginning. He is not talking here about sin as we have mistaken so many times. He is talking about something else. This is the sum total of where we have missed it, and this is the purpose of this book.

He is not talking about the result of the problem--sin, but the problem itself--self. He is talking about our ability to do life, without our works being influenced directly by Him. He is talking about life lived outside of a connection with God's voice. He is talking about how we lean on just our human natural senses and strength to live life, not Him. This is the original intent here.

We were made to live our life with a constant connection to the Holy Spirit living inside us. To repent means *"to stop, turn around and go in another direction"*. It means to obtain and use another operating system. We are to stop living by our own senses producing dead works, no matter how good they seem and live by our spiritual senses through a constant connection to the Holy Spirit's voice inside of our spirits.

The writer now says, *"if God permits"*. He says this because there has been a delay. God has timing for all of this. He has wanted to show us how futile it is to live life without His help. As a matter of fact, it is impossible to live out our true potential without Him living His life through us and us able to cooperate with Him. The only way this life, we are talking about, can be accomplished is to allow Him to strengthen us to do it. God strengthens only what is of Him. There is a glorious time coming to His church. He has taken the time to show us we are operating the wrong way.

IT WAS IMPOSSIBLE FOR THE PEOPLE TO GO INTO THE PROMISED LAND

Why was it impossible for them to go into the land? It simply wasn't time for it. He had not presented the way yet. He had not presented the operating system. Like then, I believe God has not prepared the way until now.

He said that the land and the inhabitants have not yet reached the point of iniquity that would warrant the actions needed to be taken for Him to remove them from the Promised Land. Simply put, things had not gotten bad enough yet. I believe things are bad now, because He is revealing some of the changes that have to be made right now. The times we are in are a sign that it is nearing the time to go into all He has for us--completion and the promised land of rest.

It wasn't time for the saints to reach their destiny. The *perfection* or *completion* is the promise He has for us.

NOW THERE IS A WARNING GIVEN

Once you first receive the initial stage of salvation, (Hebrews 6:4-8) and if you do not go on to perfection, you will lose the hope and faith to go on to finish your salvation. This is what the writer is talking about. You will lose the energy to go on to perfection if once you start on this road to salvation you turn back to the old system. Once you turn from your connection to Him and this process and aren't consistent, it is impossible to gain hope for it again.

I don't believe the writer is saying here you are eternally lost and will not obtain this salvation. Impossible here refers to our own ability to get it back. It simply means it will be God's doing through you, not your ability to proceed. He is saying this is His work in you, not your work.

This is the most important lesson to learn. Our completion begins and ends at the Cross.

Jesus' work is finished and He cannot do anymore for us than what He already has. He has provided all. If we do not move on then we show contempt or mock His work that was completed on the cross. He says that if we do not achieve perfection we nail His son to the cross a second time.

THERE ARE BETTER THINGS THAT CONCERNING YOU

The writer in Hebrews 6:9-12 brings a strong exhortation. If you will once again believe for your own salvation, God will not "*forget*" the energy that you have put into the kingdom of God and His people. He will remember your efforts. You have been faithful in the past and He will be faithful to you in the present. He knows our inabilities and weaknesses and will do something about it. He realizes that hope is the key.

Hope infuses us with energy in our spirit to go on. Hope will cause us to realize our destiny to be conformed into His image. Hope will bring us to the place where Christ is in us, the hope of glory!!

He is warning us not to get *"disinterested"* like the people in the wilderness did and never reach the Promised Land. People today are getting disinterested. They are living life like other people do (I John 4:5-6) and have given up trying to obtain the life of Christ. There are always *some* that will enter into the promises of God. As said earlier, if you have to, just hook up with those that are going in. The people who fell on the desert floor refused to imitate those who were going in. Don't give up!! Don't give up!! Sure we are discouraged, but the time has come now to get past this place. Why?

FOR GOD HAS PROMISED

We must be convinced on the basis of His goodness. We have to be persuaded, induced and adjust to this hope of His life working out in ours. (Hebrews 6:13-18)

This gives us an *anchor to our souls*. What does that mean? It will energize us to keep us moving on to perfection if we hope in His goodness and work to bring us there. No, we cannot get there on our own, but Jesus can get us there by His blood and the Spirit brings us to this completion he speaks of. We have to be persuaded. I am persuaded that He can do it!!

All through the book of Hebrews, the writer brings first some teaching and then stops and exhorts them to move on. Why, we have a tendency when we see our own weaknesses, to give up on ourselves and others. Here is a short list of the transitions between teachings and the exhortations the writer stopped to give those he was talking to.

Hebrews 1:1,	Hebrews 2:1	Teach - different angles and Jesus
Hebrews 2:1,	Hebrews 2:4	Exhort - don't neglect salvation
Hebrews 2:5	Hebrews 3:6	Teach - all things under our feet
Hebrews 3	Hebrews 4:11	Exhort - today if you will hear
Hebrews 4:14	Hebrews 5:11	Teach - Christ high priest

Hebrews 5:12   Hebrews 6:20   Exhort - let us get past
Hebrews 7:1   Hebrews 10:18 Exhort · don't forget beginning

John, the apostle, said it all when he said: *He Who Has This Hope Purifies Himself (I John 3)*.

Change is coming!! If you are old enough, just think of the changes the computer brought to the way we OPERATED previously. When the computer age came, it was a total and complete change, not with what we did, but how we did it. We were still making cars, providing food, educating our children and so forth. It changed completely the way we did all those things.

VI

Understanding Our Condition Now

THE SITUATION TODAY IS LIKE THE PROBLEM PORTRAYED IN THE MOVIE *THE WIZARD OF OZ*

In the movie the "Wizard of Oz," Oz was allegedly the great and all powerful wizard who had all the answers to everyone's needs. He wasn't any better off than the people he was supposed to help. He was gallant at best, but bankrupt of the true and complete cure for Dorothy's, and for that matter, anybody else's needs.

The disorder was that the needs of the people justified his very existence. If their need was ever truly met, the very reason for his existence would be challenged at best, and eradicated at worst. For that reason, he added to the problem by giving people hope without a solution. What we used to say was "*he just fudged it*". In the end though the house of cards, so to speak, came tumbling down. It was revealed that he was as desperate as the ones he was trying to help!!

THIS IS WHERE WE ARE AT IN OUR SOCIETY AND IN MOST CASES THE CHURCH

Our leaders, like the wizard, are promising cures for problems people have while having the same ones as the people they are trying to help. They know that Christ loves His church and wants it to continue to more than exist but thrive. As well-meaning as they are, they are trying to prop up the system all the while they are ignorant of the true cure, sort of like *"the blind, leading the blind"*. As it was in my own life, it stems from ignorance and not necessarily stubbornness. Little did I know how what God wanted to do would so drastically change my own life. I was nobly dysfunctional.

I am somewhat troubled though that in many cases it is not ignorance, but like the big oil companies, in the case of fuel, there is no incentive to reduce the need for fuel. The needs at hand are the very reason for their existence. Their very existence is dependent on the perpetuation of the problem. What would happen if all the problems would be cured? The stakes for changing the system are just too costly to make a commitment. Little do they know there are always some people like the people in Oz needing to be led out of their situation,

IT WOULD TAKE EXTREME FAITH FOR THE KIND OF CHANGE TO COME THAT IS NEEDED

God is fashioning change for us (Jeremiah 33:1). He loves us enough to not leave us to our own devices!! It will take the same faith as Abraham who had to leave everything, his entire way of life and his country. What we need is radical change and it's coming whether we want it or not.

Many prophets talk about revival and the great harvest God wants to bring into our world. As true as that is, there is something God wants to do first. Because of this great desire for the cure, let us not miss what has to happen first or it simply will not come. The consequences will be disastrous. My question has been and is, if God should revive His people, what is He going to bring the people to? Another loosing cycle like we had after the last revival or is there something we have never really experienced yet? I believe the latter is the case. I, for one, am writing and working on the cure-- the real permanent fix.

AS MUCH AS WE MAY WANT TO CLAIM ALIGNMENT WITH GOD, WE MAY WANT TO TAKE ANOTHER LOOK AT WHAT HE MEANS TO BE ALIGNED WITH HIM.

When we look at the times and seasons of God, often we can tell what time we are in by examining the feasts that they celebrated Israel. There was a small feast before the last great Feast of Tabernacles that represented this great harvest. It was called *"The Day of atonement"*.

This smaller feast is often ignored, but will occur just as sure as the Feast of Tabernacles (the last great feast representing the harvest). Let's not get the cart before the horse. Atonement, simply put means to put, our thoughts into alignment with God's thoughts. That has to happen for the Feast of Tabernacles (the great harvest of souls coming) to become a reality.

Without Atonement, Tabernacles is not possible. Why, because God's people must be in right alignment (atonement) before God can use them for the harvest (Tabernacle). I'm not saying the church as an institution cannot accomplish this, only individuals.

Again, an example of where we are right now is like in the movie of Oz. It is important to understanding the individual problem we have, and then maybe we can address the COMPLETE solution to that problem. In Tin Man's case, it was a heart, the Scarecrow's case, a brain; the Lion's case, courage; and in Dorothy's case, a way back home. They all, like us, already had inside what they needed and longed for. Someone just had to help to stir their faith and refuse to become some wizard to them.

We need, like Dorothy, a way back to Kansas (the Garden of Eden and God's voice). But the means of getting there is not a giant balloon ride. It is as near as our heart and far away as Kansas. Remember, Dorothy never left Kansas.

WE ARE GOING TO NEED SOME FAITH THAT GOD STILL HAS MORE TO COME AND HOLD ON FOR THE RIDE

First we need to obey His voice. We have to find it and learn how to obey it. In order for that to happen we will have to deny the old operating system (outside in). This opens the door to a whole new operating system (inside out) that will change the way we do everything. We will have to slow down first to learn how to use it and the means of slowing down is costly. Many will not want to pay the price. In order to slow down first, we must deny all distractions one at a time or simply have them taken away.

SOME OF THE EXCUSES THAT WE WILL HAVE ARE THE SAME OLD ONES:

1. It would be too **INCONVENIENT** for our leaders.
2. It is too **EXPENSIVE** to change.
3. It is too **DRAMATIC** to change the operating system.
4. It would be too **DIFFICULT** to change all the equipment.
5. It would be too **DIFFICULT** to change the laws of operation.
6. It would be too **CONFUSING** to change the standards of measurement.
7. It would take **TOO LONG** to change the operating procedure.
8. It would be too **CONTROVERSIAL** to change how we pick our leaders.
9. Our leaders would be too **DIFFERENT**.

VII

Living on the Old System

We, through the fall of Adam and Eve, now unfortunately have the ability to live life without a direct connection to God. This self-deception, living our lives without a direct connection to God, is an ability we have from the day we are born. This natural strength we are born with powers our lives from birth. Without God's blessing and influence on it, this natural strength becomes our root to failure.

We, as Adam and Eve's decedents, are born dead to the voice of God and left only to our natural five senses (touch, sight, hearing, smell and taste) to give us the knowledge and strength to live life. With this natural life a person learns over time to live by utilizing these senses for information and lives entirely by them. This person will remain dependent on his senses and live completely independent from God. As long as he is reasonably successful at living life powered by him, he will not understand his condition.

Some people get good at it like the Rich Man portrayed in the book of Matthew and some people are not so good at it and know they need something more. The better we are at living our life separated from God, the more delusional we become.

We believe we are in the proper state of being and actually receive awards and positions in life. Even in church life we can be doing good works in our own strength, disconnected from God. We will look like good people and yet be missing the fullness of life that comes from a constant connection with God. Reformation of the church will depend on God's people understanding the difference between operating in His power and operating in man's power.

IT ALL BEGAN IN THE GARDEN OF EDEN.

God created the Tree of the Knowledge of Good and Evil. It was not an evil tree, because God doesn't make mistakes. The Tree of Knowledge was dangerous because once man ate of it he did not need God's knowledge.

This tree of information gave the human being just enough to live on, but was in fact only just that, information. It was not God's voice and therefore the human remains without true direction for his life. It supports and strengthens this disconnection from God's voice and creates the delusion that humans do not need God. *"Google here we come"*. What about *"Google"*? We will discuss this later on.

This natural life or soul life with which we are born is the battle ground that we fight on every day. It stands between the world outside of us and the voice of God. Because from birth we are disconnected from God, our adversary the devil takes advantage of our ignorance of this breach in relationship with God. We can be completely innocent and have him still steal from us. It is fine with the devil if you are smart and even religious as long as you remain disconnected from God's voice.

Instead of finding how to secure God's voice, we make fig leaves just like Adam did. The purpose of the fig leaves was to cover the embarrassment of his nakedness and shortcomings. Fig leaves come in all forms. Adam knew he was missing something.

Religion for instance is nothing more than fig leaves to cover up the fact that we are not living up to our full potential and not fulfilling the purpose of God. Religion acts just like the placebos in the medical field. What was initially meant to bridge us to health is what we become dependent on to live with. In the end we become addicted to the substance to bridge us to heath and make that our very life source.

We have many different *"placebos"* to make us feel secure in the church. For me, being an altar boy as a young man, and a church leader when older served as fig leaves. There are plenty of Biblical examples. Nicodemus, the apostles and even Paul had tried them on for size. In the end they always prove to be nothing more than another testimony that we are coming up short of what God intended for us!

THE DECEPTION NOW

Often we are led to believe that this battle is just about good over evil, but it's deeper than that. It is spiritual strength over natural strength first. Then it becomes about good and evil. If we are made to believe it is just a matter of good over evil we will address our failures (sin) and not deal with the root problem (our natural life). We will continue to need the placebos that the church has offered for so long. We will find ourselves in a losing cycle of failure constantly needing prayer, altar calls, more teaching and certainly constant coaxing (preaching) to follow God's voice. We will only continue to find ourselves coming up short and messed up in our lives. I'm not just talking about sin, but self-inflicted mistakes because of the lack of guidance we need from God.

God never meant this to be. He meant us to be instilled with His voice and go on to what the Bible calls *"Perfection"* and *"Completion"* becoming ever more productive in walking with Him and helping people find Him through this life. It is the very life of Christ. It is the very key to success and blessings.

In order to win this battle we must look not only at sin, but how our natural life we are born with, this independent living from His voice, contributes to the problem. Remember, you can be a Christian all your life and still be living on this natural strength, even commended by our church leaders how good and righteous you are. No doubt you may be a good person. The question sometimes is not whether you mean well as much as what strength you are living with. God wants us on a different strength and way of living altogether. It is one that is in co-operation and connection with Him.

HOW DOES THE DEVIL USE OUR NATURAL LIFE TO DESTROY US?

The devil does not tempt us to evil as much as first appeals and manipulates us to depend on this natural life we are born with. We have inborn tendencies he knows and appeals to these appetites through our five senses. These have a powerful grip on us. They can be good tendencies as well as bad ones. He is not particular and will use whatever he can.

The point is these tendencies and desires can be used to distract us from God's voice and therefore lead us off the path of life God has for us. That's what it means when we say he *"Tempts us with evil"*. It's a distraction. But it isn't just the thoughts that we are thinking, it's our very strength too!! He wants us to depend on our natural strength. He knows if we continue to live on this natural strength that we will eventually make mistakes and fail. We were never created to live from this strength alone, but by the power of God. Basically, he wants us disconnected from God. Sin will automatically come.

The church as an institution has made the problem about sin. It is treating only the symptoms of the problem. People say, if only we repent of our sin we will then be able to live life with God. Not so, it is only the beginning. There is so much more to this. It is like diagnosing a person with a disease and giving them a medication that makes them feel better while not curing the problem. It keeps the church in business because they keep coming back for more. The church needs to be about our Father's business curing disease not treating symptoms.

There is only one way forward and that is to deal with the root problem. God came to earth to fix it in the person of His Son. He came as a Son of God to bring many sons to a life completely connected to Him. Hebrews 1 explains the mission of Jesus. Jesus came not only to bring us to this life but to take away the material inside of us through faith. It is that material in us that gives our adversary something to work with therefore distracting us from God's voice. It is in the Bible called the natural man, or what the Bible calls the flesh, the very strength we live by. It often comes in the form of compulsions, urges, pressure, pleasure or obligations. These things are the way the devil distracts us from God's voice. It happens every hour of every day.

THE STRENGTH OF OUR NATURAL MAN IS THE BATTLEGROUND

You may be sinless, but if you are not selfless (rid of this dependency on your natural strength) you will have a very hard time living for God and many people will be lost in this world as a result. The Lord looks for us to be submitted to Him in order for Him to finish His work in us. He wants us to hear His voice not just for our sake, but for the sake of those we come in contact with. The objective in Christian salvation is to become totally selfless and dependent and connected to God the Father in order to fulfill our purpose.

It is to have this natural strength reined in and under the control of our own spirit. I am not saying God's control, He doesn't control us, I am saying controlled by our own spirit. Our spirit is empowered to do so by the Holy Spirit. Proverbs says: *"A man that has no control over his own spirit, is like a city broken down and without walls"*. If that is the case then we can be a city with walls and fortified by controlling our own spirit. We see people all day long in this condition. This is an exciting time we live in. We are going to see people who know how to rein in their spirit to cooperate with God!!

THE CHURCH HAS BEEN ALL TOO SATISFIED WITH GOOD FLESH

What is *"Good Flesh"*? Good flesh is attempting to do God's will in this natural strength. It is trying to live for God in our own strength while being disconnected to the very life and voice of God. All too often even after being born again as a Christian, we leave His strength to begin to once again live on our own natural strength. God wants us to overcome this tendency. God wants us to be able to continually be connected to Him by reining in our natural life and the control it has over us.

Before we are born again we may have faith in God, but we are totally disconnected from Him. It isn't a matter of sin, as much as living apart from the life of God. Sin is certainly important to deal with, but being sinless is not the ultimate goal. The goal is to deal with this natural life that is the root of sin. It is that self-dependency that allows the devil and our own compulsions and tendencies to drive and manipulate our lives to do what is against the will and nature of God. We find it in every compulsion we have from sports to religion to eating.

It isn't just the sin, but the compulsion that causes us to be disconnected from Him. It keeps our attention away from God and to an inward gaze to ourselves. We will discuss this at length later on but it is important to know the root of our problem. Treating it by continually denying it is not the answer, curing the problem and the root of the disease is. Jesus came not just to show us our problem, but to bring the cure.

FIRST THINGS FIRST

The first thing that has to happen to us when we are born without God and dependent on our natural life is to be convinced of our failure. Like mentioned earlier too many of us are too good at living in this original state and many never are convinced of this root of failure. That is the tragedy for so many people. They never really fulfill their purpose.

That's what preaching was originally meant to accomplish, it was meant to *"convince us of sin and self"*. Too many for too long have paid a dear price and some the ultimate price for not coming to this knowledge. The knowledge of sin and self is simply coming to the knowledge that we cannot live apart from God completely successful. We will be distracted by our own inability to co-operate with God.

In our born again experience we first become frustrated with our own abilities and failures and then become hungry and in some cases desperate for more. This becoming frustrated is so very important and is manifested in many different ways. But we must remain hungry to walk in connection to God and His voice.

Often we think it is a one time experience but it is to be a way of life. Continuing to be convinced of our inability to live without God is something we are challenged with our entire life. This is the process. Our natural life and strength decreases, then the distractions decrease and God's Holy Spirit can come through the "iron curtain" of our own natural strength that has been built up all our lives.

When born again (our initial contact with God) we merely obtain the potential to enter into spiritual life and training. He takes His spirit and puts His spirit in us. We will explain the process of salvation from beginning to end in the following chapters of this book.

THE ONLY WAY OUT FOR US IS DEATH

It stands to reason if the voice was lost in the Garden of Eden and the failure of the human race came through the fall of Adam and Eve, then a return of God's voice is the restoration of mankind.

Simply stated salvation is when we finally realize we cannot live without the voice of God and then get re-connected to the Holy Spirit. The unfortunate thing is this natural life we have continues to plague us and interrupt God's voice even after our initial salvation experience. It must be dealt with in salvation and continually be dealt with our entire Christian walk. That's what Jesus came to do, make a way for that to happen to us continually. We must decrease in our natural strength while at the same time increase in our connection to Him and His strength.

The cross and resurrection is the way to the life worth living in God's power and knowledge. Just think of it, dead people don't respond to outside distractions through their five senses. In addition we have a person inside, God himself through the Holy Spirit with His five senses leading us. It is a constant. Once we taste of this new life it is impossible to go back the same way. We are going to bring to reality how we can co-operate with the Holy Spirit 24/7. We are going to obtain this way of life, because Jesus came for that very reason!!

WE NEED TO LEARN HOW TO HAVE SPIRITUAL LIFE

Many people receive through His salvation a better attitude, but they don't know how to receive the better life. We need to be returned to the voice of God permanently, not just through a prayer life in different parts of the day, but a walk with Him. Remember, we actually become the garden with that voice of God from the inside out. The voice is now inside of us. (Ezekiel 36) But first we must examine where we are now and where we need to go.

Many people and yes, many Christians are stuck at different conditions of living. Some are satisfied and some are not satisfied as to where they are living. I am going to address these different conditions and hopefully you will find where you are living and know and understand the next level and how to get there.

IT FIRST STARTS WITH KNOWING JUST WHY GOD GAVE US HIS SON JESUS

One thing we do know for sure is that we have a model, a prototype, that God has given us in Jesus. In the Old Testament we had the law to state what we are to look like. We didn't seem to get it through the law, so God sent His Son Jesus as the *"Prototype"*. In chapter one of Hebrews is says that, "He was the *Firstborn among many sons*".

Jesus came to <u>REVEAL</u> just who the Father was and looks like;. He came to <u>REDEEM</u> us from sin, <u>PREPARE</u> us for the Holy Spirit which is His voice, and most importantly show us a <u>PATTERN</u> for how to continue to live with the Holy Spirit.

He was willing to not only go to the cross but provide for our natural strength to decrease by bringing us to the cross by our faith in Him, so we can, through the strength of the Holy Spirit, deny our natural life and strength daily and follow Him. Get ready for an awesome trip!!

All of the apostles knew all this. Peter for instance saw the transformation that Jesus would go through. He saw the prototype on the mountain while walking with Him when He was alive. Jesus was transformed before their very eyes. Mathew 17:1-5

Later Peter said, (II Peter 1:8), *"If these things are yours, you will never be unfruitful in the Knowledge of Him. Never stumble"*. We can cooperate with God. We can destroy the works of the devil, and we can take back the dominion God intended for us humans to have all along.

But first we must know where we are at and where we need to get. Let's look in the next chapter at the big problem with our walk. We will define and describe dualistic thinking and the different conditions we live in.

VIII

A Description of Dualistic Thinking

Among the thousands of modern conveniences we enjoy, are cordless devices: cordless drills to cordless sanders, self-contained devices to slice your roast or trim your whiskers, portable telephones, rechargeable flashlights, etc.

The principle is: use it until its power is exhausted, return it to its *"Base Station"* for recharging, and then repeat the cycle. When it is finally called home to gadget heaven, you give it a decent burial and pick up a new one.

One point to make is that the base becomes the all important part of its life. Without the base the appliance is useless. Where is the incentive to create something that doesn't need a base for recharging? Devices with a self-contained energy supply.

THE INSTITUTION OF THE CHURCH HAS BECOME OUR SPIRITUAL BASE.

With this kind of thinking the church becomes our spiritual base; and we, the people, are the cordless devices. When the base is the most important part of the tool, it has a need to be sustained. The majority of the work is to just *"keep it going"*. When people hold this philosophy of life, they remain completely reliant on the base station. If the base station (church) is lost or broken, they (the people) are ready for the trash bin. This of course demands that we secure the base station for without the base station the devices (people) become useless.

God never intended this base station mentality to replace our day-to-day personal walk with Him. People who approach life via the *"cordless"* method get charged up during church services and then live life in their own natural strength until they run out of charge. **Their source for living life is themselves, and they are vulnerable to slowly losing their cutting edge and finally grinding to a halt.** Thus the trip back to the base station to charge back up, if they can find one that works for their brand.

As a cordless Christian (living in the false security of our own talents, strength, even spiritual gifts), we can give our life the old college try all week as the pressures of the world volley us off its walls like a racquetball. Then *"Praise God"*, it is 5:00 P.M. Friday; we have made it through another work week. We see Sunday as the opportunity to plug into our *"spiritual base station."* We even speak of church attendance as *"**getting our battery recharged to face another week.**"* It is just another dose of exhortations and motivational energy to get through yet another week. **Then we repeat the cycle.**

There is nothing wrong with some encouragement through fellowship of the believers. In some cases that is exactly what we need to get us through a season of dryness. But to become and propagate this dependency stunts the believer's growth towards spiritual maturity and eventually reaching *completion*.

This mentality also diminishes, if not dispels altogether, the purpose of the church as an institution to teach people how to stay plugged into the Lord personally all day long. Instead the altars at our churches are filled with people re-dedicating their lives each week, trying to run up the batteries because all week they use up the power they got from the base relying on their own power. Their failure is often looked at as a failure of commitment. *"If only I can get more committed"*.

God calls this trusting in the *"**Arm of Flesh**"* (*2 Chronicles 32:8*). We depend on ourselves; calling upon God only in times of need, and often feeling like His calls are being forwarded to His voice mail. We then wonder why our spiritual life is so dry.

This was not the original purpose our Creator had in mind for the church in the beginning. We need the better model. The church as an institution has a purpose, a very important purpose. The institution of the church is very much still needed, for training, equipping and affirmation, in order to make people sufficient on a new power source, the Holy Spirit.

THIS APPROACH TO LIFE PARALLELS THE WAY MANY LIVE FOR YEARS

In this system of operation, there is little difference between Christians and non-believers. We can be a pastor, do apostolic work, missions, etc. and Jesus can definitely be the focal point of our lives, but **He may still not be the very LIFE source.** If God somehow removes the power of our own flesh (what is called our natural life), we will collapse like a punctured balloon because that is our only source. This is when most people come to embrace their need to trust in and rely on God. They become acutely aware how futile it is to *"do life"* without God's power every day.

In the word of God it says: "Thus says the Lord, 'Cursed *is the man who trusts in mankind and makes flesh his strength . . .'* " (Jeremiah 17:5). Cursed here implies utter failure to live life on our own.

As time rolls by for the person who lives in his own strength, the joy of the Lord they knew early on being in His presence is often supplanted by wearisome religious duty. They take comfort in the knowledge that they are going to heaven when they die, but they know nothing of resting in Christ on earth as they live. **"While a promise remains of entering God's rest, they seem to have come short of it"** (Hebrews 4:1). Many don't fully understand the principle that Christ is to live His life through us while we rest in His sufficiency. We need to deny our natural strength and let Christ rise in us daily.

Come to church, receive a word, and get your spiritual recharge. This is what we have learned from those who were supposed to bring us into something more. **It keeps the business of building and sustaining**

base stations going. It started centuries ago and continues in every Christian denomination today.

What am I saying? There is much more to the Christian life than what many believers experience today.

Regardless of my opinion, the important thing is to recognize that God says there is more to the Christian life than the cordless variety offers. He calls it ABUNDANT LIFE. This is the church's mission,--to promote and bring the people into this ABUNDANT LIFE. He said out of our bellies will flow living water. We are to be the source of life through His abiding presence in our lives, from the inside out. (Ezekiel 47:4) We are to be a self-sustaining river of life.

THERE IS A BETTER WAY: CHRIST EXPRESSING HIS LIFE THROUGH US

The secret to an overcoming life lies in understanding how to stay *"plugged into Christ"* moment-by-moment, as opposed to operating as if we had a rechargeable battery. Jesus called this *"**abiding**"* in Him (John 15:4). He is the way, the truth and the life.

The Christian life is accomplished just like it was acquired: by faith. We are to simply believe that Christ is our life because God says so (John 14:6, 15:5; Romans 15:18; Colossians 3:3-4), and then act like it's true. As we can see, there is a huge difference between trying to live our lives for Christ versus Christ living His life through us. It is the difference between failure and overcoming. The difference is the source of energy we are operating on.

Being continually plugged into God makes us ready for the fresh revelation of how to trust Christ within us as even more than Savior and Lord; **Christ is to express His life through us.** When God lives His life through us it is like nuclear fission. God in us creates new energy, sufficient in supply for all our life.

Also, as we have Christ in us, He gives us the wisdom, knowledge and understanding of just how to use any knowledge we may have. Just how to do that, is the mission of our church leadership.

CONTINUOUS DEPENDENCE UPON CHRIST (ABIDING LIFE) BOTH NOW AND FOREVER IS THE MESSAGE OF THE GOSPEL.

Somehow the Deceiver has managed to sweep this truth through the cracks. He's convinced us that we're to *"live our lives for Jesus* as if we were so important that He needed our help instead of allowing Jesus Christ to express His own life through His own body--the individual members of His corporate church. The enemy knows if we remain in our natural strength long enough, we will run out of our own resources. We will make the self-inflicting mistakes that will bring us to complete failure.

The question to answer is, if Christ would live an overcoming life through us, would we know how to cooperate with Him? **Would you do so?** That's what experiencing Christ living His life through us is all about. Each individual person as a part in the body of Christ is to *"live out"* his unique identity by being totally dependent upon the Head, Jesus Christ, as his life. Independent living is not Christianity; it is a man-made caricature of Christianity.

We must trash the unbiblical belief that an independent, self-reliant life is worthy of our pursuit, even noble and virtuous, and learn how to live in total dependence upon Christ within us to express his life through us.

How does that happen? As the Scripture simply says: ***"I must decrease, He must increase"*** (John 3:30). The Scriptures describes it this way, ***"I am Crucified with Christ, never-the-less, not I, but Christ lives in me, and the life I now live, I live by the faith of the son of God who loved me and gave himself for me"***, (Galatians 2:20). If you notice it says: *"I AM crucified with Christ"*. It is a mindset of constant death to our ability to live apart from God in our own self-sufficiency. This is what he meant when He said: *"Pick up your cross daily, and deny yourself"*, (Luke 9:23). It means to deny this self-sufficiency of our natural self and depend entirely on Him all day long.

The Scripture goes on to say: *"never-the-less I live, not I but Christ lives in me"*. We are to live in His sufficiency as He strengthens us in our inner man and that strength works its way throughout our being. The

Scriptures say: *"The Holy Spirit works in us both to will and do of His good pleasure"* (Philippians 2:13).

May the Lord bring us into this kind of spiritual life today!!! But before He can, we need to know on what level we are living on. Yes, we all are living on different levels of spirituality depending on the training we have received.

Let's now look at the different levels people live on and find ourselves in which level we are on now. Let's go on to *perfection* and *completion* walking with Him and go on to be fully successful through His strength in fulfilling His purpose for our lives and bringing others to Christ-like living.

IX

The Different Levels We are Living on

Due to this dualistic thinking we have continued to live on several different levels in our Christian walk. We start out with the first level of faith and hopefully move on to walk that faith out to fulfill our destiny. However, in most cases just like the wilderness journey described in the Bible, it takes much longer than it should. It takes time, trial and error, yes; but it was never meant that we camp out at each level as the Israelites did. The Israelites' journey to the Promised Land took forty years when it really was only an eleven day journey. Because it took longer than it should have, an entire generation did not make it in and many of the next didn't see any rest at all.

This is where we are today as God's people. There is another generation preparing to go into the Promised Land. There are still others who are struggling to keep up. There are those like Joshua and Caleb who say:, *"We are able to go up and take the country"*. With the proper teaching and encouragement we can shorten the time needed. May the Lord help us!!

The world is dying and needs us to move on to *perfection* and do the real work of the ministry which is to bring in the final Harvest of people. This is none other than the Feast of Tabernacles. We need to stop being sidetracked by seeking different religious exercises and work that lead us nowhere. We have no more time to wander in the wilderness while our bones bleach on the desert floor and the world goes to hell in a hand basket.

Here are the different levels of Christian living I have found. I'm sure you may see different "***variables***" in these different levels of living. We need to find where we are living and progress to live the life worth living.

THE FIRST LEVEL:

<u>The</u> <u>Person</u> <u>Remains</u> <u>A</u> <u>Perishing,</u> <u>Miserable,</u> <u>Believer.</u> Other than their faith in God there is not much noticeable difference between them and a non-believer. That's just it, they believe in God, but do not enter the kingdom of God (the spiritual realm promised by God) or what the Bible calls "*Eternal life*". They have not been born again, experienced the touch of the Holy Spirit or the infusion of life from Him.

They may be very religious but are filled with their own ways and the consequences of them. Jesus said "*you must be born again to enter the kingdom of God.*" (John 3:1) Being born again is when we become conscious of His presence in our spirit. It is when God's Spirit comes and touches and visits our spirit. Jesus is the way to the life of the unseen kingdom of God and a personal relationship with the Father.

Nicodemus, one of the religious rulers of his day (John 3:1), was in this position when Jesus met him. So was the apostle Paul and so was Cornelius (Acts 10:1). They actually believed in Yahweh and considered themselves servants of God, but they like all of us needed more. They needed a connection to God and thus His voice. And for every honest man or woman that needs more I have to believe, according to God's goodness, they will receive more if they ask Him to meet their need. May God help them to reach that point in their life and then may they find someone who knows the Holy Spirit who can lead them to spiritual maturity.

Early on, Paul, the apostle, was on this level. He had faith in Yahweh, and was taught God's ways and laws at the feet of Gamalie. Gamalie was a great Jewish teacher of God's law. But Paul ended up persecuting the early Christians while thinking he was doing God service. God had to knock him off his horse, blind him and get him some help from Ananias who knew what this was all about. Thank God Ananias went to Paul when told to!!! Paul believed on Jesus, was filled with the Holy Spirit and the rest is history.

Cornelius in the Book of Acts in Chapter 10:1 was also in this position. He did have faith in the same God and pleased him. He was living at the level of faith and knowledge he had. Cornelius prayed and his prayers were heard by God. God answered by sending him to Peter and showing him more of the life God has promised us. He showed him Jesus and a better way. The Holy Spirit fell on him and his entire family. We all need God to show us more. We will see that Peter was on another level trying at the same time to hear God and do His will all the while not hearing Cornelius knocking downstairs on his door. This represented the very thing Peter was seeking God for and could not hear it.

THE SECOND LEVEL:

<u>The **Born Again Christian.**</u> When a person is a *born again*, they are forgiven of their sins and their eternal life is secured (the heaven and hell issue is solved) and now they have *"The ability to know Him"* (God). They have made initial contact with God spiritually. (John 17:3)

This person though continues to live a dualistic life. We described the dualistic life in the last chapter. Again, a dualistic life is living one way (prayer, bible reading, going to church, etc.) while depending on their own natural strength and ways to accomplish their everyday life. They cannot maintain a connection with God until secluded or someplace alone where they are not distracted by things and events coming at them through their five senses.

There is a vast separation between the way they operate and the way they are supposed to operate, which is an abiding life fully connected to God 24 hours a day. (John 15:1)

This is known in the Bible as a *"carnal or fleshly believer"*. (I Corinthians 3:1) Simply put these are people who live a dualistic life. They are spiritual beings since being born again, but live in their natural strength disconnected during most of their day.

To be "*carnal*" is to live strictly by their five senses and influenced by outside circumstances depending on the natural life they were born with. They remain disconnected from the voice of God inside, due to the rhythm of the five senses and reacting to them. They have not gone on to learn and live the spiritual laws in Christ. They are not delivered from compulsion to respond by outside influences and pressures.

This person reaps the same consequences in life as other people do because while being born again they are still not practicing the *spiritual laws* for the life promised by God. Because a person has the potential to be spiritual doesn't mean they will ever be spiritual. There are laws to being spiritual that must be kept and most people have not learned them.

THE THIRD LEVEL:

The Spiritual Christian. This is a person who goes on to grow into a *Spiritual Christian.* . They have learned through practice of the spiritual laws (Hebrews 5:11) to stay connected to the Holy Spirit from the inside out and show forth the fruits and gifts of the Holy Spirit in their lives continually. They have no need of proof of this life. This person's life, work, demeanor and actions speak for them.

If you notice here none of these statements point to any position in life or ministry as a measure of one's spirituality. This addresses the inside of a person not the outside position in the institution of the church.

This is where much of the disappointment and cynicism has come from in the church today. Leaders that have position outside, but lack the spiritual mature walk we are describing.

Because the Lord loves them He allows them to run out of their own strength bank needing a better way of living. In Christianity there has been all too much in the showroom and not enough in the stock room.

I'm going to devote my life to helping people go on to this third level. I'm going to teach them how to complete their spiritual life. This life is to be evident through both the gifts of the Spirit and the fruits of the Spirit, all nine of each in every life flowing. This is the evidence of a mature spiritual Christian person.

This is the purpose of the teacher in Christ, to help teach in such a way that the saints are *"perfected for the work of the ministry"* (Ephesians 5:11). The gospel is a gospel of attraction and it's time to reflect His character in all we do.

X

Receiving Our New Operating System

As stated previously, we, like the computer, have an operating system from the time we are born. When God created Adam and Eve, He created them with this system of operation. He gave to them five senses and His voice in the garden as a guiding force.

He knew Satan would come to disrupt His communication and relationship with Adam and Eve. God knew from the beginning that Adam and Eve would need direct contact with Him from the inside to be successful in life. Why didn't He give him something better from the start? Adam and Eve would first have to choose to let God into their lives or their relationship would be mere mechanics and not a matter of free choice. Love is not love without free choice. Oh the patience of God!!

Satan at one time was God's prized creation. After Satan's fall, Adam and Eve were the replacements. That is why Satan is called our adversary. We will deal with him and his actions specifically throughout our writings.

THE WHOLE WORLD NEEDS THIS NEW SYSTEM

The Gospel presented not just a new life, but a new operating system. We need the new operating system for that new life to work and we need it to work now!! We were meant to live and walk *"as Jesus walked in the earth"*. (I John 2:6). This means on the system he lived on, not necessarily the very same work He did. It's the system of how we operate that needs to change not just the activities we do.

The result is that it restores mankind to the voice of God and brings rest from outside stimuli as the Scripture puts it *"freedom from agitating passions, fear and moral conflicts"*. (I Peter 1)

We are reaching to the end of this age where I believe we are going to be introduced to this way of life. It was in the Bible all along. It is called *completion* or *perfection. It is the only life worth living.*

Paul, the apostle, desired to present every man and woman as complete. He lived and breathed to see this happen. (Colossians 1:28)

In the next book, we will take a look at what completion looks like and why we have not come into this way of living. The paradigm we will use is the very picture God intended all along, the temples or tabernacles. Jesus spoke of his body as the temple of the Holy Spirit. (John 2:20).

Paul said we were the temples of the Holy Spirit. (I Corinthians 3:16), *"Know ye not that ye are the temple of God, and that the Spirit of God dwells in you, if any man defiles the temple of God, him shall God destroy; for the temple of God is Holy, which temple you are.* This opens up a whole new understanding to God's people.

In the Life worth Living series of books, we will see the human being as the temple and study its laws from this prospective.

Ezekiel 44:10-12 *"You son of man, show the house to the house of Israel, that they may be ashamed of their iniquities: and let them measure the pattern, And if they be ashamed of all that they have done, show them the form of the house, and the fashion thereof, and the goings out thereof, and the comings in thereof, and all the forms thereof, and all the ordinances thereof, and all the forms thereof, and all the laws thereof: and write it in their sight, that they may keep the whole form thereof, and all the ordinances thereof, and do them. This is the law of the house; Upon the top of the mountain the whole limit thereof round about shall be most holy. Behold, this is the law of the house."*

We can then learn to operate on the system God intended for us in order to fulfill our destinies as His sons and daughters. Success can only come through these laws, and through these laws it will come.

This is an exciting time we live in. It is exciting because I can see the answer becoming clearer and clearer. In our next book, you will be given a clearer picture of how to obtain The Life worth Living. Some serious challenges are ahead for our world, but I am convinced without these challenges we will not be prompted to make the changes necessary. If we do meet the challenges, the results will be unimaginable. We will finally learn to live our lives with the inner voice of God present making the way for the Holy Spirit to live through us. Our aim is to equip the saint with a walk worthy of Him.

He who has this hope in him purifies himself!! (I John 3:3)

Made in the USA
Charleston, SC
14 June 2014